WEIGHTLIFTING

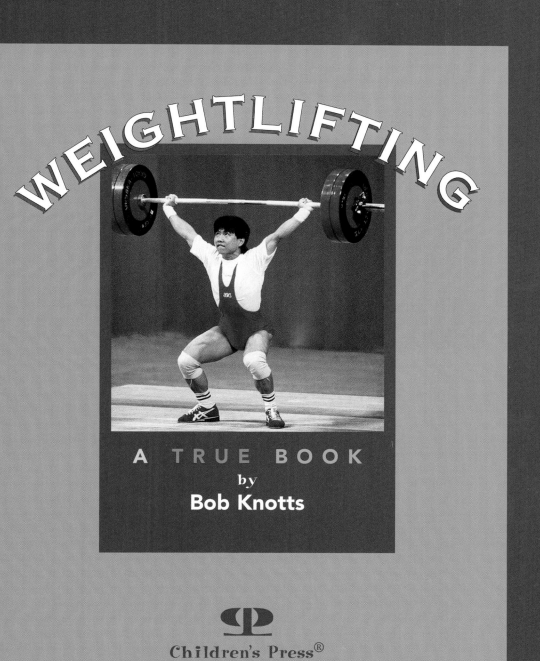

A TRUE BOOK

by
Bob Knotts

Children's Press®
A Division of Grolier Publishing

New York London Hong Kong Sydney
Danbury, Connecticut

A woman weightlifter

Reading Consultant
Linda Cornwell
*Coordinator of School Quality
and Professional Improvement
Indiana State Teachers
Association*

Author's Dedication:
To Jill—Thank you.

**Visit Children's Press® on
the Internet at:
http://publishing.grolier.com**

Library of Congress Cataloging-in-Publication Data

Knotts, Bob.
    Weightlifting / by Bob Knotts.
        p.   cm. — (A true book)
    Includes bibliographical references and index.
    Summary: Describes the history of the sport of weightlifting, as well as
the training, equipment, rules, and techniques involved.
        ISBN 0-516-21067-X (lib.bdg.)   0-516-27032-X (pbk.)
        1. Weight lifting Juvenile literature. [1. Weight lifting.] I. Title.
II. Title: Weight lifting   III. Series.
GV546.3K56   2000
796.41—dc21   99-15089
                                                                              CIP
                                                                              AC

GROLIER
PUBLISHING

Contents

Lifting as a Sport

You have probably lifted many things during your life. Maybe you have lifted only light objects such as drinking glasses and milk cartons, or pencils and paper. Or maybe you have helped someone lift heavier objects such as a table and chairs. Lifting things

is part of everyday life for most people. We usually don't even think about it when we lift something.

But some very strong people lift things as a sport. These athletes lift heavy metal weights. That's why their sport is called weightlifting. Competitors try to lift as much weight as they can. The man or woman who lifts the most weight wins.

It's hard to believe how strong the best weight-lifters really are. If you weigh 95 pounds (43 kg), the strongest

Weightlifters are strong enough to lift more than their own weight.

Olympic weightlifter could lift six of you over his head at once! That means he can pick up 580 pounds (262.5 kg)!

But there is much more to weightlifting than just picking up heavy weights. Weightlifters must learn many skills so that they can lift those weights safely. They must train hard to gain strength. And they must follow the rules of their sport.

One thing about weightlifting is important to remember: never try to lift weights without

A weightlifter training with his coach

proper training first! Reading books about weightlifting isn't enough. It's very easy to hurt yourself while weightlifting, so you need someone who knows weightlifting skills to show you how.

Weightlifting History

Long ago, strong muscles were more important than they are today. Men protected their families with strong muscles. They caught animals for food and fought off enemies too. Strong people lived longer than weak people. Maybe this is part of the reason why men

An ancient Greek stone carving showing a man lifting a heavy weight

have tried all through history to prove who was strongest.

Chinese writings from five thousand years ago tell about soldiers who had to pass weightlifting tests. The ancient Greeks showed their strength by lifting heavy stones. Later,

Weightlifting was included in the first modern Olympic Games in 1896.

weightlifting competitions were common in European countries such as Scotland. In 1896, weightlifting was included in the first modern Olympic Games.

Both men and women lift
weights in competition today.
Women were first included in
the world championships in
1987. They competed in the

Women and men
compete separately
in weightlifting.

An Olympic gold medal is the dream of every competitive weightlifter.

Olympics for the first time during the 2000 Summer Olympics in Sydney, Australia. The most important thing any weightlifter can do is win an Olympic gold medal, the first-place award.

The Olympics have had some great weightlifters. One of the greatest was a Russian named Vasily Alexeyev. He was a huge athlete who weighed more than 300 pounds (135 kg).

Vasily Alexeyev

During one Olympics, Alexeyev was seen eating twenty-six eggs and a steak for breakfast! But Alexeyev was strong too. He won two Olympic gold medals and set seventy-nine world records between 1970 and 1979.

Not all great weightlifters are big people, however. One of the best is a man who is very small but also very strong. Naim Suleymanoglu of Bulgaria is under 5 feet (152 cm) tall.

But he has won three Olympic
gold medals—the only weightlifter ever to do this. He weighed
just 132 pounds (59 kg) when he
won his first gold medal in 1988.
He lifted almost 420 pounds
(190 kg) over his head!

Rules and Equipment

In weightlifting, athletes compete against other people who weigh about as much as they do. This is because heavier athletes can usually lift heavier weights. In Olympic competitions, men are divided into eight weight categories, or groups.

Weightlifters compete against other weightlifters who are about the same weight.

Women are divided into seven weight categories.

The athletes lift a barbell, a long, heavy metal bar that has round weights at each end. The bar alone weighs

44 pounds (20 kg). Each weight weighs as much as 55 pounds (25 kg). Two circular clips, called collars, are placed over the bar at each end to keep the weights from falling off. Weightlifters often wear wide, leather belts to support

The weights on a barbell are held on by circular clips called collars.

A weightlifter often wears a wide, supportive leather belt (left). Chalk gives weightlifters a better grip on the barbells (right).

their back. They also may wrap bandages around their knees and wrists for extra support. Weightlifters sometimes put chalk on their hands to give them a good grip.

Both men and women do two lifts during competitions. The total weight of these two lifts becomes the final score. This score is used to decide who wins. One lift is called the snatch. The other is the clean and jerk.

The snatch is done very quickly, without stopping. Weightlifters bend over and grab the bar with their hands far apart. Then they pull the bar up toward their chest and

The snatch lift

drop down into a squat. As
they squat, they raise the bar
over their head. Finally, they
stand up and hold the bar overhead with straight arms. They

The clean and jerk

must hold it without moving until the referees, or officials, signal to lower the bar.

The clean and jerk requires two separate motions. Weightlifters can pick up more weight in this lift than in the snatch. First, weightlifters

grab the bar with a wide grip,
then pull it up toward their
waist. Then they quickly squat
down, just like in the snatch.
The difference is that the
weightlifters now raise the
bar only to their shoulders as
they squat. Then they stand

up and prepare for the second half of the lift.

After a moment, weightlifters push the bar overhead and straighten their arms. They use their legs to help push upward as they do this. They bring their legs together and must stand without moving until the referees signal to lower the bar.

A third lift, called the press, was dropped from the Olympics after 1972. The press was like the clean and jerk—except for one thing. Weightlifters were not allowed to use their legs to help raise the bar overhead. They had to push it up with arm strength alone.

Both the snatch and the clean and jerk require great strength and lots of practice. Always remember: Don't try to do these lifts unless a trained weightlifter has given you lessons first!

Powerlifting &

Some types of weightlifting competitions aren't in the Olympics, but they're very popular. One of them is called powerlifting. In powerlifting, the only thing that matters is how much weight an athlete lifts. This sport has fewer rules than Olympic weightlifting.

A powerlifter preparing to do a bench press

Bodybuilding

Bodybuilding is another form of weightlifting. Bodybuilders lift weights to increase the size of their muscles. In competitions, the winner isn't the strongest man or woman—it's the person who looks the best.

A women's bodybuilding competition

A men's bodybuilding competition

How to Win in Weightlifting

Weightlifters spend many hours in the gym each day training with heavy weights. They also eat a special diet that helps them stay healthy and develop strong muscles.

Like other athletes, a weightlifter must have a strong mind

A weightlfter in training

Weightlifters must have the right mental attitude to succeed.

as well as strong muscles. Mental strength helps weight- lifters lift heavier weights.

Their chances to win are better if they believe in themselves and truly want to win.

In competitions, weightlifters first have three chances to do the snatch. They can't win if they don't complete at least one snatch. This is because the winner is the person who lifts the heaviest total weight in both the snatch and the clean and jerk. Next, a weightlifter has three chances to do the clean and jerk.

Some weightlifters shout when they lift weights.

Often, weightlifters shout when they lift weights in competitions such as the Olympics. This is because shouting can give a person extra strength for an instant.

But there are some things weightlifters must not do. For example, they can't touch the floor with any-thing except their feet. A lift doesn't count if a knee or any part of the body bends to the floor.

Weightlifters are also not allowed to touch their arm or elbow to their leg during a lift. They must be able to hold the weight without leaning it against their legs.

Some weightlifters begin training when they are very young. In the United States, boys and girls can enter weightlifting competitions at any age if they have an expert coach. But these young weightlifters must train a lot

A sixteen-year-old competitive
weightlifter from Hungary

before trying to compete. To
become strong, weightlifters
must work hard and have lots
of patience.

Weight Training

Another type of weightlifting is popular among people who do not take part in weightlifting competitions. It is called weight training. Some doctors and fire-fighters and even writers do this type of weightlifting. So do athletes in many sports, including football and baseball players.

Many athletes, such as professional boxer Evander Holyfield, use weight training to strengthen their bodies.

A woman training with light weights

Weight training is exercising with weights. People who do this don't try to lift as much weight as they can. Instead, they do exercises over and over with light weights in order to strengthen the body. A strong body is usually healthy and looks good. A strong body helps in playing most sports, too. An athlete who trains with weights can run faster and throw farther.

Of course, weightlifters do weight training to get strong for their sport, too. They train with weights until their muscles are large and powerful. Only the best make it to the

A woman weightlifter in competition

Olympic Games and other top competitions. And only the strongest win gold medals and other awards.

This is the dream of serious weightlifters everywhere—to break world records, to win Olympic medals, and to prove they are among the strongest people on Earth.

The thrill of victory

To Find Out More

Here are some additional resources to help you learn more about weightlifting:

 **Books**

Greenspan, Bud. **100 Greatest Moments in Olympic History.** General Publishing, 1995.

Kent, Zachary. **U.S. Olympians** (Cornerstones of Freedom). Children's Press, 1992.

Lund, Bill. **Weightlifting.** Capstone Press, 1996.

Perry, Philippa. **Olympic Gold.** World Book, 1996.

Wallechinsky, David. **The Complete Book of the Summer Olympics.** Little, Brown & Co., 1996.

Organizations and Online Sites

International Olympic Committee (IOC)
http://www.olympic.org

Find out about the organization that runs all Olympic Games.

International Weightlifting Federation (IWF)
http://www.iwf.net

This page can tell you about the organization that supervises all international weightlifting events.

Pan American Games Organizing Committee
Pan American
Games Society
500 Shaftesbury Blvd.
Winnipeg, Manitoba
R3P 0M1 Canada

The Pan American Games include one of the most important weightlifting competitions other than the Olympics.

United States Olympic Committee (USOC)
Olympic House
One Olympic Plaza
Colorado Springs, CO
80909-5760
http://www.usoc.org

The United States Olympic Committee supervises Olympic activity for the United States. Its website includes everything you'd want to know about Olympic sports, past and present.

USA Weightlifting
One Olympic Plaza
Colorado Springs, CO
80909-5764

USA Weightlifting supervises weightlifting events for United States athletes.

Important Words

ancient existing a long time ago

barbell long metal bar that weighs 44 pounds (20 kg) and is used to hold weights

bench press pressing weights up with one's arms while lying on one's back on a padded bench

clean and jerk one of two lifts in weightlifting competitions, performed in two movements

collar metal clip placed over the bar to keep weights from falling off

competition any activity in which someone tries to defeat someone else

snatch one of two lifts in weightlifting competitions, performed in one movement.

squat to crouch on one's heels, with the knees bent and the weight usually on the balls of the feet

Index

Meet the Author

Bob Knotts is the author of five True Books on Summer Olympic sports. He also writes for national magazines, including *Sports Illustrated, Reader's Digest, Family Circle, Travel & Leisure,* and *USA Weekend.* He has worked as a newspaper reporter as well as in radio and television. He has been nominated twice for the Pulitzer Prize. Mr. Knotts lives with his wife, Jill, near Fort Lauderdale, Florida.